S0-FDJ-645

River Voices

To Sue –
with
much
love.

D

River Voices

The Poets of
Stuyvesant Cove Park

Published by
The Stuyvesant Cove Park Association
Box 178
Peter Stuyvesant Station
New York, NY 10009-0178

To order copies of this book,
please contact us at the address above or
check our web site: www.stuyvesantcove.org.

The watercolor of Stuyvesant Cove Park
on the cover is the work of
Ila Bonczek.
The cover design is by Peter Garland.

Copyright © 2006 by
The Stuyvesant Cove Park Association, Inc.
All rights reserved
Printed in the United States of America
by Kanter Press, NYC

ISBN 0-9785289-0-5

CONTENTS

FOREWORD

The Poets of Stuyvesant Cove Park constitute a diverse group of poetry lovers: some write poetry as an avocation, while others have been published. The group began meeting in June 2003 after the announcement of a series of poetry readings on Thursday evenings—a series dedicated to and named for the late Steven H. Rosen, one of the founders of the Stuyvesant Cove Park Association. Mr. Rosen was both a lover and a writer of poetry.

On each of those Thursday evenings, two poets read from their work. In a very short time our original plan of honoring a beloved person brought together individuals who, through their love of poetry, formed bonds of friendship and mutual support. After the first summer, we met once a month with an open invitation to the public to join our circle to share their original poems, or a favorite poet's poem, or just to listen and enjoy.

The shared appreciation of poetry, the love of the written word, and the inspiration offered by Stuyvesant Cove Park itself sparked a growing desire among a smaller group of the "regulars" to put together an anthology of their own poems. After much discussion it was decided that each contributing poet could choose three of his or her works for inclusion in the anthology. Poets whose poems had appeared in our newsletter, *The Cove*, were also invited to contribute.

We are extremely pleased to bring you *River Voices*, our first anthology of poetry from the Poets of Stuyvesant Cove Park.

We are indebted to several people for their contribution to the production of *River Voices*: Peggy Unsworth, a former English teacher, who typed poems for those who lack a computer; Phoebe Hoss, a poet and professional editor, who edited the poems and compiled them into this anthology; Frieda Lane who helped with proof reading; Ila Bonczek, who earlier participated in the park's design and construction, for her watercolor of the park on the cover; Peter Garland, for the cover's design; and Wendy Byrne for the book's typesetting.

We are also indebted to the public and private individuals, too numerous to mention, who fought for many years—through Community Board 6 and Citizens United Against Riverwalk—to save our waterfront from the mega-development known as Riverwalk, and who helped to transform a local eyesore into the award-winning Stuyvesant Cove Park.

Thanks as well to the Board of the Stuyvesant Cove Park Association for underwriting this anthology and to the Friends of Stuyvesant Cove Park who, by their financial contributions and volunteer efforts, help to sustain our park. We are grateful to Solar1 for offering us a welcoming meeting space. And lastly, we thank you, the reader, for supporting *River Voices* and the Poets of Stuyvesant Cove Park.

Joy Garland, Executive Director
Stuyvesant Cove Park Association
April 16, 2006

River Voices

ROSE BERNAL

Scene at Stuyvesant Cove Park

Late morning in late August.
Clustered buildings, stylized columns
of varying heights and hues
weigh down the shore.
The slapped cove is smitten with birds.
A black cormorant spreads his wings
to dry. A seagull circles, glides,
and beats his wings for life.
Another screeches by. Sparrows
and mourning doves peck at the seaweed
slime. Blue sky, puffed intermittently
white, blanches at the edges, as if
about to disappear. Droning helicopters
and seaplanes hover, circle, and undulate
on the water. Traffic noise an anodyne.

Love disconnected from personal balm,
now free to go on a wider arc.

Hibiscus,

overgrown crinkled lavender gauze,
wine center staining pink striated seams
out toward cupped edges furled over the
waxy spine of the stamen flecked
with yellow filaments resembling
a tiny round hairbrush

flaunting indolence, redolent insolence
flopping dreamily, nodding off

while looking at the waves continuously
sucking at the cove outcrop facing it.

Tompkins Square Park and Environs

What can there be

in a tree gnarled thick?
Wavy spidery branches
weighed down, drooping,
and early fall?

In an old man, jaunty, ambling?
Another steady on a bicycle;
the juggler on the circus platform
in the background clamor?

In the silence of the marble
graveyard? Pillars, pedestals,
and columns; inscriptions
commemorating those gone?

What can there be
except an image and an aura
of the living always performing:
the dead always in peace?

ESSE CHASNOFF

The Lost August

Walking through the foyer to the closed door,
Following you as you swing it open,
But it closes behind you.
And when I have opened it
        there is another empty foyer,
And you walking toward another door
        and the door following,
Again, the door closes behind you.

At the summer garden
The trees droop into the pools,
        the sculptures stand around
        a Henry Moore woman
And a woman lying near the pool.
The music pounds
Struggling to realize itself,
Strangulated.
Hohvannes, Gideon, Ned Rorem, Corigliano—
All living composers.
"666" lights blinking on the top corner
        of the tower.
You helped to build that tower
Now it's near the anniversary of your death.
I sit listening and watching children
        walking quietly.
Their silhouettes blend with the trees,
        dipping into the pools.
Lovers caress.

People look at the performers and listen attentively.
Two pianists tearing at the strings.
The towers reach up.
Traffic roars.
The shadows of the leaves speckle the concrete.
Quietly selling sandwiches, soda,
      the men stand by.

The Chain

From a small city in the Ukraine
A poor Jewish mother, Ethel, struggles with poverty,
      a sick husband and son.
She sends her only living daughter to America
      to escape the encroaching dinginess and dread.
The daughter, Taube, feels the crush
Of unrelenting yearning and isolation
      in a strange land.
Later, she will have a daughter, Ezhele.
Ezhele will have Yitte Etele,
      who will have Tova.
Tova also has to fight to survive.
She has Taube-Ezhele-Yitte-Etele genes
      floating around,
Dancing to bolster her strength,
Little figures holding hands,
Swaying and straightening,
Flickering and enduring.

Summer Town

On Thursday, the day was so steamy
Streets sweated.
I plodded through the sidewalks, melting
Vapors issued from the cracks in the concrete.
As I headed for First Avenue, my head
        came off with an obsession.
The neighborhood seemed so seedy.
In the morning there had seemed to be
        a greater parade of homeless people
        in varied postures.
The fat lady was shouting epithets.
A deranged man banged furiously on a dust bin.
My heart sank.
How could Manhattan be saved?
Then, on Sunday, balm arrived.
It was a hot afternoon but there was
        a pre-storm breeze.
Girls were out with their fellows.
Ukrainian, Mexican, Israeli, Yemenite coffee shops
        seedy but homey, inviting sitters.
Moishe's kosher bakery offered an onion rye.
I stopped to buy, and the old lady with a
        Hungarian-Bronx-Jewish accent
        of long ago waited on me.
Oh New York! You did not disappoint me.
You brought me down, then you brought me up.
You are hateful, terrifying, dangerous,
        calm, peaceful, life-giving,
                and beautiful!

ESTHER B. COHEN

Sweet Pinks

Sweet pinks upon the windowsill
      Pinker in the dark air, still
Searching for the light
      Not concerned with might or right
To be as beautiful in one fair day
      Content to pass and gently fade away.

The Alone Together

Endless—the streams of people
      moving—moving
         off the train
           together.

Where to? Together
Unaware—unmoved—unstirred
      by one another.
Moving together—away
      from each other
Never having seen—felt—
      known
         the alone
    Alone together.

Botticelli

First time beheld—
     A garden fair—
A light in the cold gray
     winter air

Green feathers—
     green eyes light—
Orange circles round
Yellow mask—aqua crown
Red gray blue in the
     long tail gown

Flamboyant antics—action fun
Cooing sounds—
     A searching stare
Of course she knew that
     I was there!

Oh yes, she came home
     with me that night
Is that what is meant
     by love at first sight?

MARILYN DRISCOLL

The Visitors

Dressed conservatively in iridescent gray
And not expecting company,
Pigeons waddled on the paved walkway
Pleased to feast on plentiful crumbs,
Content with wings sufficient for their needs.

"Uh oh. Look up! See who's coming to town!"
Some salty show-off cousins
Swooped in from the shore.
Gulls, whose soaring style and noisy calls:
"Here we are!
Look at us!
Welcome us!"
Caused embarrassment and envy,
A flutter of discontent among the landlubbers
Who normally find their shorter wings
Ample for emergencies or for dutifully heading home.
In a critical huddle they complained:
"Don't some know that wings are for emergencies,
Not for riding high on every breeze?"

Preminiscence

Preminiscence is the conscious
Appreciation now
Of someone or something
That will lose
Its immediacy
And one day become
Only a memory
Eligible to be
The stuff of reminiscence
When the reality
Is no longer here
To be enjoyed.

On the M-23

He was young, thin, perhaps a little pale.
His white cane helped him board the bus.
Almost he sat in someone's lap.
"Excuse me, please," he said,
And found a space nearby.
Apartments for the blind are on my route.

Another boarded, husky, hairy, also young.
His white cane was a hockey stick.
Taller than he, it scraped the lights
And his backpack bulged into the space of others.
No "excuse me" words were heard.
Chelsea Piers is also on my route.

Copyright © 2004 by Marilyn Driscoll.

10

MARY FORDHAM

A Hunter in the Evening

In the high desert where little rain falls,
monsoons bring heavy downpours
and hand-built swales guide water
to fruit trees yearning
to anchor themselves in dry rocky soil.

Yet asparagus flourishes in a fenced garden
in view of scattered sun-bleached cattle skulls
and large boulders with ancient petroglyphs.

In the evening, when lights appear
in the swale-builder's house,
a shadow moves between two boulders,
a golden arrow gleams in the moonlight
and flies

to strike a wild boar,
that falls amid saltbush and sage.

Desert Artemis has proven her skill.

She leaps over the boar and runs to her sister's house,
where they dance through the night
as their drumbeat fills the desert air

and coyotes feast on wild boar.

Bird Call Reaches

A bird call reaches
over the treetops of the jungle,
seeking, seeking its mate.
Then another calls and another sings,
weaving a tapestry of bird song.

In the city humming and rumbling sounds
fill the spaces between tall buildings,
reaching over roofs and water towers.

She pounds the taro root, chanting,
talking with the birds.
She pounds the taro root, chanting.

In the city air conditioners roar,
restaurant exhaust fans drone,
horns honk, sirens wail, brakes screech,
cell phones ring.

She sits on a rock in the middle of the stream,
singing to the waterfall.
She sits on a rock in the middle of the stream,
calling her wandering pig.
The river flows past her and the water falls on rocks,
weaving a tapestry of water sound.

She sits on her rock singing
a song about her village.
It guides her to the lone swaying palm,

alerts her to the small creek that dips,
warns her of the waterfall ledge,
reminds her that her ancestors speak
through the spirit tree.
Will her brother return?
Will the butcher bird call him back to the jungle?

In the city few birds greet the sunrise
or serenade the sunset.

If only a rainstorm would wash away the city sounds.
If only I could sit on a rock in the middle of a stream
and sing to a waterfall.

Copyright © 2005 by Mary Fordham

Bashenis Still Life*

A mandolin, a lute, and a violin lie
together on a Persian tapestry of rich reds
covering a Renaissance cabinet.

There, too, a Venetian globe
with hand-colored continents
sits atop three large leather-bound volumes.

The cabinet stands before a sienna-painted wall
where amber velvet drapery
is pulled to one side.

Under the violin are glimpsed
parchment music sheets,
their corners curling.

Traces of fingers wiping across
the dusty mandolin, lute and violin
suggest the passing of time and
instruments forgotten.

*"Evaristo Bashenis (1617–1677), the preeminent still-
life painter of 17th-century Italy, is best known for his
haunting poetic paintings of musical instruments. During
his lifetime Bashenis—himself a musician—amassed an
impressive collection of instruments and musical scores.
The artist would arrange these into carefully choreo-
graphed compositions for his paintings, presenting novel
and daringly foreshortened views of the instruments."
(From the Metropolitan Museum press release on the
exhibition of Evaristo Bashenis 11/17/00–03/04/01)

JOY GARLAND

Prayer Energy

I have a cell phone.
When its battery is low,
I plunk it down into its charger.
It sits there silently in its cradle,
Allowing new energy to enter and recharge it.

When my spiritual battery is low,
And I know it,
I sink myself in prayer,
Inviting the Spirit to enter and recharge my soul.

But it's very hard for me, to just be
Silent, inward.
I'm itching to get to my computer again,
To record donations, to acknowledge donors,
To return calls, to finally liberate myself
From the accumulation of clutter.
To just be, is hard for me.

I need prayer as I need food.
Why do I resist it?
My prayer, Lord, is to increase my faith
In the power of prayer to move mountains,
To save the Earth, to bring peace and healing,
To unclutter my mind and my apartment.
This prayer energy from above,
Is it the energy of Love?

The East River

The poet speaks,
"They said you were dead,
No life could possibly live in you.
One half inch of rain
and down the drain
comes the storm's wet passion
out of five sewer outfalls
mingling with heavy metals, PCBs,
and whatever garbage was
thoughtlessly thought gift to you.
Can the wet womb of first life barren be?"

The river speaks,
"Ask the blue crab that swims under the pier
and the hungry gull that scavenges my waves.
Ask the striped bass, the flounder, the eel,
and the cormorant that harvests among the rockweed.
Ask the children who plunder the periwinkles
and the homeless man who fishes
and washes away life's grime.
Ask the barn swallows that skim my shores
and the ducks that dive my depths
without disappointment.

I am wounded but still alive
because some of my children have heard my cries
and came to my rescue.
The politician's pen proclaimed pollution's end,
and fines were levied to renew the blue
of heaven mirrored in me from 'sea to shining sea.'
America, America, God shed God's grace on thee
to mend thine every flaw with regulator's law
that soon may cease to be.
Let the outrage come and overcome the
        deregulator's greed
that would sacrifice our health for wealth
and open wounds to bleed.
Let the Congress and the President meet the
        present need!"

Winter's Dream

When winter covers the sleeping earth
    with a soft white blanket of snow,
While daffodil bulbs slumber and dream
    of warmer days below,
The larva of the butterfly in its
    chrysalis hung low
Cannot foresee the miraculous change
    that it will undergo
When spring returns and brings to birth
All that is waiting in the frozen earth.
And our souls, too, will soon revive
Reclaimed, reborn, free, and ALIVE!

LYNN GREEN

Fairy Tale

We give our families sources of nutrition far beyond food.

I have only one carrot for you, my love,
And no bananas.
What will I feed you after you
plow the fields or
crunch the numbers?
What will I feed you
after you cure the sick or
shoot to the moon?

I will feed you my poems—
luscious strawberries dipped in wine
dripping chocolate into crystal glasses,
and peaches plucked from fairy trees,
ripe juices staining your fingers.

I have only one orange, my sweet little ones,
and the jam has run out.
What will I feed you
when you run to me hungry?
What will I feed you when
evening ends your play?

I will feed you from my stories—
fairy castles and girls in pink dresses,
brave knights riding their horses,
dinners of spun sugar
to last all the day.

Double Nickels I

Time was when a woman could
sit a bit and reflect,
while she slowly transformed
into a wise old sage
with grandkids rollicking
around her plump feet,
her stories creating a line in the chain
of gentle memories.

Time was when she could savor
her accumulated wisdom
and keep her secrets,
quietly smiling into the shadows
of remembered winter nights
and warm summer days,
the crunch of fall,
the drizzle of spring.
Life rolled on her tongue,
settled into her heart,
and let her breathe.

Time was when her SOUL flew free,
soared to the sky,
floated to earth,
and settled to the gentle
rocking of the waves.

Time was when she could
sit a bit and understand
that her seasons pass with
the color of the leaves,
the snow and the rain nourish her,
and she brings forth flowers
that bloom into eternity.

Double Nickels II

But hold on—here comes granny
stuck to her cell phone,
sporting 2-inch spikes
with hair of many hues,
off to the gym to keep that old
(did I say old—heaven forbid!)
ticker going beyond any natural lifetime.

We're gals off to have fun,
to show the world that we still
got what it takes
(despite our backs, knees, and tennis elbows),
that we can keep up with the best
(despite our stomachs, livers, and bladders),
and that we're standing on the neck
of old Father Time,
cutting off his air with our $100-dollar Reeboks.

BARBARA GURMAN

Street Living

no bills
no checking account
no bank statements
no withdrawals
no deposits;

no shopping, cooking, cleaning
no telephones
no cell phones
no call waiting
no caller ID;

no obligations
no responsibilities
no appointments
no schedules
no deadlines;

no TV
no baseball games
no football games
no calls to make;

no toothpaste
no floss
no deodorant
no warm showers
no warm baths;

what to do?

go to soup kitchens
go to homeless shelters
talk, smile, laugh
live in the present
meditate.

Miracles

Birth is a miracle;
a book is a birth;
new ideas are creations;
creations are births.

Life is a miracle;
love is a miracle.

We are all miracles;
we are divine;
we are extraordinary;
we have no limits,
only our minds think we do.

We can and do exceed our highest expectations;
our potential is unlimited;
we keep stretching and growing,
and going beyond what we thought was possible.

What if nothing is impossible;
what if there were no such word as impossible?
That would be a miracle.

Forgiveness

I forgive others easier
and more quickly than myself.

Why am I more forgiving of others?
Why do I have more empathy for them?

No matter what they do, or how they do it,
I seem to be able to understand their behavior.

Maybe I'm guilty of the
I-know-better way of thinking.

My standard of living is more advanced.
Am I better than they are, whoever they are?

Do I need to forgive myself, or anyone,
because we're all growing, evolving?

Can I feel the light of God in myself, in everyone,
regardless of my behavior or theirs?

We Are One.

PHOEBE HOSS

Minor Phenomenon

Like some gorgeous snail,
a rainbow creeps all but
imperceptibly across
my wall, illuminating
for a moment—never staying, never
staining—jutting corner,
grave bowed head of embroidered
Chinese heron in its frame, books
on their shelves. It's simply
a beam of light shattered
by the crystal on my windowsill.
It's simply a small visual
delight I'm used to. But today,
as I lie here reading, it arrests
me. I think beyond that luminous
trail, beyond the sun
powering it, to the nearer
body, the humble, the
enormous one—so obvious,
so invisible—that's simply turning,
turning, bearing me and billions
like me, also obvious,
also invisible, through
each of our days.

Out of the Cement Hives of Manhattan, Simple Miracles

Framed in the elevator door, they'd
step out into my life, briefly
punctuating it—that full stop
in the foyer as we'd chat about the classes
they were taking—pottery, Shakespeare—
or whom I was editing or some new
iniquity of the government. I'd met him
in the laundry room one Saturday night, learned
he hailed from Indiana, had been a union
organizer; her later, born New Yorker, public
school teacher, her mother Jewish
from the then Ukraine.
Over the years I came to count
on meeting them, my elderly
neighbors, would in the street seek out
Joe's squared-off face under faded hat brim
so like my father's: Lili's cheeks plump
as a girl's, like my mother's, and her eyes deep-set
like hers, too, though not a flashing bluejay
blue but dark—dark as olives, dark
with anger after Joe's death last fall, fauve
dark, intense as the paintings of hers wreathing
the walls of their apartment, which I saw for the first time
       this March,
on the afternoon she died.

"We love you. We love you,"
they used to say on parting—startling me mysteriously,
moving off some familiar template, moving
to fill some absence I recognized

only when they'd gone, the absence
of those simple words those other two—immured
in the immemorial fear of spoiling
their children—never spoke.

I love you, Lili and Joe,
I love you, I say now
on parting—as I, too, never, ever,
to the other two.

In memory of Lili Sweat (1911–2003) and Joe Sweat (1916–2002)

Sightings in Stuyvesant Cove Park

Swarthy, short, in jeans,
t-shirt, he's like the other
fishermen; like them, rod-bent,
intent; like them but
for that bonnet on his head: that bonny
bonnet, its white straw gleaming
in the sun, its full white bow
trimly tied in back.

Cormorant diving: svelte
in black, chic as Chanel,
fruitlessly aped
by one shaggy black
buoy.

Scuttling by, street-smart
sparrow, her beak clamped
tight on a crumb as big
as her head.

What's that rat-
a-tat-tat, machinegun
rattle? Boy on silver
scooter skimming back
and forth, over and over,
detonating one long strip
of bubblewrap.

Brown carapace clutching
brown carapace:
horseshoe crabs snug
in erotic spasm.

Plucked from Hiroshige
print, if not escaped
from someone's apartment:
the white parakeet
plump on small yew branch.

That swathe of silk—gray-blue and softly
shirred and pleated—that binds
Brooklyn to Manhattan reminds
me of a dress I loved till some early boyfriend
ripped it off me.

Suddenly, against the rocks, waves dash
and splash, exulting for no
known reason.

Small figure, bright breasted:
the genie of this place, garlanding
it with joy.

For Joy Garland

ANNE LAZARUS

Sandra's Willie, A True Story

A black and furry little stray
Wandered down my path one day.
He looked so lost and so forlorn
In Williamsburg where he was born.
His kitten purrs and kitten cries
I couldn't resist those big green eyes.
A tiny tyke, an orphaned waif
I took him home where he'd be safe.
With love and care, good music too
He prospered and he grew and grew.
He'd climb and jump and hide and run.
Oh, what a day of kitty fun!
He hath a game he doth adore
Called "Throw the objects on the floor."
He plans his moves with stealth and skill.
He's very clever, Good Old Will.
Willie had a friend named Fred.
They ran and jumped. One chased. One fled.
But Fred is now a co-op cat.
No playing in that one-room flat.
Poor Willie of his friend deprived,
But street-kid Willie he survived,
And Mistress Sandra now deploys
An arsenal of treats and toys.
Do Willie's antics ever lag?
He slept inside the garment bag.

Car Pool

The tribulations of a pool
Will test each person's verve and cool:
The passenger with lots to learn
Who faults your every move and turn,
The one who opens windows wide
Insuring us the coldest ride,
The member who is always late
While all the others fume and wait,
The one who plays the rock and roll
Exacts a painful mental toll.
Now peace and quiet descend on me,
I've opted for the B.M.T.

Elite

I sit by the window and gaze at the trees
For I am the master and do as I please.
And if you don't serve me an haute-cuisine treat
I'll scream and I'll yell till I wake up the street.
I'll eat and accept of my favorite food
Provided I'm in a receptive good mood.
Oh, I am the lord of this posh habitat
For I am an East Sixties Siamese cat.

PAMELA MACHADO

Summer Sounds

What does the ocean say to the sand?
The stars to the night sky?
Clouds as they pass the day?
The moon is always so far away.
Only the wind talks to a breeze,
Summer grass whispers to earth,
Rain and sun play in the leaves
On trees that are always alone.

Nothing

Nothing takes up so much space.
Nothing has no color.
Whenever there is nothing there
Neither is there any sound.
Silence is a precious thing.
It doesn't stop the mind.
Just slows down thoughts and wishes,
Leaving nothing to disturb,
Giving peace and rest and calm
To all around who listen.

After Sorrow

I remember simple pleasures—
A Saturday night dinner after
a green market day,
Going to Cold Spring Harbor
just to sit by the harbor,
The chores for me apart from yours,
The regular work day,
Simple joys like holding hands,
Being part of a couple.
These I know.
The last touch of your hand.

DAVID MAYER

Cove Scenes
A Dialogue with Our Feisty Neighbor—The East River

Me: River! River! Burning Bright!*
          Target of Sun's molten light!
          What unwritten tidal law
          Weds your water to our shore?

He: World-class stream? I'm tops, a star!
          Global gene stream? Best by far!
          Family tree? I'm New York's pride!

Me: Would you, could you be my guide?

He: Sure, let's go for a river ride!

          The sap that runs in my family tree
          Matches the ocean's salinity.
          I'm an arm of the Atlantic Ocean,
          Its salt—my fresh—make quite a potion!

          I'm an estuary, slave to the Moon,
          The pull of gravity calls the tune,
          A two-step segue, day and night.
          In . . . out . . . high . . . low . . . a killer sight!

          Bestuary of the Year? I won it!
          Without your help, I couldna done it.

*Thanks, W. B.

I dream of changing my nothing name.
    East! A compass point! Whom can I blame?
    Historians tell me that in 1524
    A daring Italian explored my shore,
    Named Giovanni da Verrazzano.
    Wish I'd been named for that paisano!

    I'm doing m' best to please you all.
    Just let me know if I drop the ball.

    Arrivederci, pal, gotta flow now . . .

In You I See

In you I see
fate's gift to me.
My private Sun,
my Venus, Mars,
all shooting stars.
My warming light,
my day, my night.
My age, my youth,
my dream, my truth.
One heart, one life.
Eternal Wife.

(These rhyming lines are a
way to express in words the
inexpressible delight of a
loving union —David Mayer)

The Battery at Noon

An ardent sun scatters crushed diamonds
across the quivering skin of the East River.

Below me, incandescent wavelets
press against the base
of the shoreline walkway.

A solitary wild duck climbs awkwardly
across a rampart of rocks
between narrow beach and river.
Afloat, it serenely paddles toward open water.

Above me the Brooklyn Bridge reverberates
with the thunder of its traffic.

Time resumes its flow. I immerse myself
in Pier 17's human tides.

EVE NETHERCOTT

Sounds in the Knight

When a husband doesn't listen,
      A wife becomes resigned;
She knows that half her chitchat
      Goes past his egghead mind.

He never likes advice—
      His tune is, "Don't tell me!"
So she lets him do things his way
      And lets the matter be.

But the time she really suffers
      The burden of abuse is
When he neglects a chore, and then
      "You never told me!" his excuse is.

Lovely Lady's Chatter

She reads the literary page—
The music and the art news
So she can stand around and quote
Not hers, but all the smart views.

Inevitables

Come what may
There's night and day;
Spouses bicker,
Children play.
World goes on,
So does dinner.
I grow fat,
My wallet thinner.

Good listeners are more popular
Than those of us who talk a lot,
But we who talk have lots of fun
While the listener has not!

I find it taxing
A diet maintaining;
Therefore, I'm waxing
Instead of waning.

STAN RAFFES

Dancing with the Moon

A restless midsummer night
in Cape May, New Jersey.
The offshore breeze at midnight
parts the lace curtain
in my Victorian bed and breakfast;
the full moon shines, luminous,
prancing over the ocean waves
past the boardwalk,
inviting me to dance.

I step out on the patio
in my open-toe Birkenstock sandals,
inhaling the stars, the moon,
the salty air
until my mind does a moon dance.

My memory quicksteps
through my childhood in Flushing in the 1950s
way before the World's Fair, Vietnam, the high rises,
when the side streets looked like
the fragrant woods
they were named for—Ash, Beech, Cherry—
and us up in our tree house,
made from orange crates and scrap wood.

Memories tango through my adolescence,
when I was totally breathless, enthralled

by my beautiful French teacher,
in tight skirts,
with a radiant smile,
where I strained
to hear her every word in French,
every syllable, noun, verb,
a miracle.

Now, in 2005, waltzing in place
with nostalgia and regrets,
here, in my little
Hansel and Gretel cottage
in Cape May.

Think of Pablo Neruda,
who painted his poems
with sensuality, mysticism, and moonlight
and one particular poem, late in his life,
"Today I Have the Moon,"
where he said,
"Those who say I have lost the moon—
they lie."

Smoke

My Uncle Sam
smoked only the finest
Cuban cigars,
long, elite, brittle, decadent

Hand-rolled tobacco,
treasured like rare orchids, each
cigar encrusted
in a 24-carat gold band.

Sam displayed them
like Incan treasures
for his guests in Larchmont;
smoked each cigar like an emperor
as he glided silently upstate
each evening on the Major Deegan Expressway,
from his store in the South Bronx, in
his long, sleek, black 1972 Imperial,
its silver fins, medallion
gleaming under the arc lights of the highway.

On sweaty summer nights,
he loved the rush
of the highway breeze through his power windows
while concentric blue smoke rings
wafted out into the night air
like the old Lucky Strike billboard
on Times Square.

He died from lung cancer
four months after my Aunt El's funeral,
sunk into the soft, leather couch
of his den like a sultan.

The empty bullet casing
from his last cigar
on his Moroccan
end table

next to his prized Nat Sherman humidor,
like a display case at the Met,
hand-rubbed oak, delicate Swiss dials.

Tip of his last Cuban cigar still glowing;
held in his chubby fingers
in a death grip—
the ghost of a smile
playing across his pale face.

The Crimson Tango Dress

Discovered it again
buried deep in your cedar chest
meticulously wrapped in pink tissue,
the red ribbon still perfectly preserved.

Seemed to crackle
right out of the dress box,
springing to life,
becoming electric again,
dancing wildly,
powered by an unseen electric current
            in that moody old attic,
in the shafts of light
that winter afternoon, so many years later,
doing a wild Argentine tango
on the padded hanger.

The slinky tango dress
almost weightless,
blood red, dizzyingly hot,

slit up to your thighs,
racing wildly up your taut dancer legs
before coming to a screeching halt.

1970 August—Miami—95 degrees—hurricane season—
Starlight, National Ballroom Dance Championship.
You seemed on fire with the tango—
your partner, José, all muscle, movement,
costume skintight, black and white silk,
Cuban heels.

You dazzled, 1,000 handsewn sequins
sparkling, three and a half minutes of immortality.
You were precise, passionate blurs of motion,
pounding on the hardwood, each precise step,
six months of exhausting practice.

You, incandescent, like Evita,
tangoing, pounding out Argentina's
long bloody history
in a brief, wild, passionate marriage
of accordion music—heart, soul, determination.

Now, held up to the light,
red ribbon—still perfectly preserved,
your crimson tango dress, still dancing,
rich with perfume and musk,

under the attic's hurricane
ceiling fan
on a steel hanger
in the cold light of this March afternoon.

DOROTHEA SCHER

Status Quo

Beautiful young man on the bus.
Dazzling eyes.
Tousled black hair.
Your profile makes me throb.
Even when I was young,
I doubt I'd have been
smart enough,
dumb enough,
curvy enough
for you.

Now I'm invisible
to beautiful young men.
Nothing's changed.

Sleepless Nights

As a kamikaze or a bullet
hurtles to its prey,
so the pelican plunges
straight down
toward a fish, unaware,
slipping through transparent water and,
in a wink,
not.
So, you,
night after night
skewer me in my dreams and
never
never
never
never
let me wiggle away.

Now and Then

Suspended between a blanket
of gray clouds and wan sky,
sealed in an airbus,
movement is imperceptible.
One endures the vacuum,
exits through similar jetway
into identical airport.
How many gas stations, car lots, drive-ins
before a difference is revealed?

In another time
scenery passed.
Voyages were not silent.
Trains hooted.
Steel on steel measured miles,
clickety-clack.
One lurched toward the toilet,
saw railroad ties through a hole.
No need to flush.
One left parts of oneself
on the landscape.
It took two to loosen latches,
wrestle windows up for air
on hot summer days.
Cinders bedecked one.
Insects sucked in,
caught a ride in windblown hair.
Each station unique.
One knew, stepping from the coach,
it was somewhere else.

JUDY SCHERMER

Down Time

In this odd place of
Repose from work and
Everyday usuality

As I fight myself for
Being in
Suspension

I get to reside in
Times of
Off-the-beaten-trackness

Getting acquainted with my
Undermutterings

Jus' Dancin'

Slap Slap Slap
My flat soles go
Snap Snap Snap my
Thumb 'n
Middle Finga

Chin peekin' over
Ma shoulda

Nostrils flarin'
Head tippin' down
Eyes up and flirtin'

Down-There's
Goin' round da clock and
Back de udder way

Cells of jelly gawn
Quiverin'
Rubbin ma
Neck
Rufflin' ma hay-er

Hey whut's goin' on?

B. B. King's playin' da
Blues

Dat's whut!

If You're Ethnic

If you're ethnic
But want to fit in
Pick your suit of manners
And behold
You can pass with the rest of them
And your secret's un-told

If you're ethnic
Effervescing with the zing of life
Venturers will draw your nectar
And take every inflection
Foreign phrase
Symbolic gesture
And drive it through a P.A. system
To make it
Larger than it is

If you're ethnic
And you're pressed for a two-step
Could you dance a kazatzka
And be yourself
Instead of them?

(This poem was originally published
in the *UNDP News*, May 1997.)

49

BETSY SHEPARDSON

Hearthside Writing

Twelve days has Christmas
Twelve months has the year
Twelve weeks to chill the bulbs
Before they warm in the sun.

Shall we plant Ice Follies,
Dutch Masters, or Yellow Suns?
Dancing daffodils to brighten
January, February, or March?

What shall we have for
The white of winter? The
Green gray leaves of a clump
Of daffodils twist and turn

Catching the sunlight. One
Of the four flowers hangs back
Curled shut as if it were
Cold. Others open to the sun.

They rustle in the cool
Breeze. They brighten up
A Special Party. Spring sunlight
Kisses them—ready for the garden.

Happiness in Movement

Let's go!
Precious playful pony
Optimistically waiting

Harnessed into a dark place
Trying to find a way
Back to nature.

Grounded, solid
Blue and black pony fun
Yeeha!

Ready for a ride.

Montana Heritage Barn

The long brown wooden slats
Of a small unpainted homestead
Barn—its boards weathered
With stories of long ago.
The old tin roof shines in
The sun, sparkling against the hills,
The green pasture and purple mountains.
White, wispy clouds
Drift in the broad blue sky.

Inside the barn are three stalls
And a small tack room.
One stall for the range horse
That can find its own way and
Fetch a rider home in a blizzard.
The smaller stalls for goats
Yielding goat's milk—for it is a
Rodeo horse! The cattle shed abuts
Both partner and neighbor.

Nearby stand the cottonwoods
Giving shelter; for when
Horses buck and jump in autumn
The weather will change.
There will be cold and snow.
But a rainbow in the evening
Means the next day
Will be good weather; folk stories
Tell us that the sun will come.

In the night, a locomotive whistles,
We see many twinkling stars
And rain appears, as well as Pegasus
For his hooves thunder in the skies.
We see his golden bridle
Lying in the old tack room
Before Aurora mounts him to
Bring forth the dawn—
Or Apollo rides Pegasus, bringing the sun!

ALISON CARB SUSSMAN

Bronx Boy on the Express Bus

. . . There's a kid next to me, all wired up with music
       and stuffing his pale unblemished face with candy.
Boys.
They're all arms and legs at that age.
I feel hampered now, unable to write, imprisoned.
He produces yet another box of candy from his zippered
       jacket pocket.
How much candy can a kid eat?
This kid is shaking the box of candy and I hear
       the candies rolling around and the sweetish smell
       makes me hungry.
They're some sort of crunchy cherry and chocolate candies,
       yechh. Just the sort of thing kids love.
Doesn't he know all his teeth will fall out if he eats
       that crap?
Wish I could eat it. Wish I could be a kid again,
       a boy especially, cramming my mouth full of candy.
He casually rolls the candies out on his palm and tosses
       them into his mouth, flinging back his darkish hair.
There's something beautiful about it,
       something beautiful about this young stranger . . .

Jones Beach

I stretch and move out of bed.
My bones are cold; relics in a glass case;
    my teeth all silver with bits of food
        gummed in them.
I'm at my desk in pajamas.
Can I live in the world and write about it?
My heart beats slowly,
    my weight like a great white whale.
I stare at the bowl of water I have placed on the desk,
    wait for poems to float like bodies to the surface.
Now, only memory comes.
Phil and I at Jones Beach:
March. Smashing surf.
Wind beats at our clothes like the fists of the child
        we do not have.
Gulls.
Us forever in the moment—
We walk toward the beach as the sky darkens,
    look for nesting plovers in the delicate brush sprung
        from the dunes.
We find pieces of driftwood, a toy shovel.
The gulls surround us and shriek when we take out
        our sandwiches.
Dune grass bends under the wind, swishing its skirts.
I wear shapeless pants and a bulky coat.
My husband plods ahead of me, scans the sky with his
    binoculars.
The light shreds itself against a house onshore that we will
    never live in; breaks up, flees into safe corners.

Hustler

I saw the same
hustler in the doorway of the apartment building next
       to that
X-rated video store off Second Avenue.
It was cold.
He wore a heavy jacket, and a scarf
wrapped around his neck and lower face.
I knew he was a hustler
from the way he stood. He looked young,
       in his 20s maybe,
with clear corn-fed American skin.
He stared out
into the wet streets, splashed with lights like
       postmodernist paintings.
I call this painting *Traffic at Night* the road the shapes
       of cars with their lights,
slashes of white, dashes of red on the pavement's
       slick surface.
A man in a black jacket streaked toward him.

PEGGY UNSWORTH

Summer Sunday, England, 1941

Mum keeps watch from her upstairs kitchen:
clouds scud above swaying poplars;
suburban garden holds her child at play.

Eight years old, I totter in her Cuban heels,
socks balled up to fill the toes.
Serve meals to deserving dolls
now propped against the wall.
The menu? Michaelmas daisies for fried eggs.
Garnish? Silver-green rosettes—
rose-tipped bromeliads from our rock garden.

Our Mum scrubs up and dusts us down,
a labor fueled by her off-key song.
Wreathed in steam, she cooks our meal:
chops cabbage, whisks Yorkshire pudding,
bastes beef and turns the spuds.
I stir the simmering Bisto.*

No fridge,
Cold water sink,
Bare wooden table:
Her cupboard shelves hold everything.

Bisto is gravy powder in the United Kingdom.

Just Desserts

On a dish, washed dusky Boscs lounge rampant.
Replete with bouncy stems,
they sprawl 'mid Red Delicious,
jostle yellow fellows. Is this all show?

Awkward and bulbous,
like fat thighs they betray cellulite.
Granular, pocked, implacable,
once bitten, will they gush juice?
Taste one and know.

Ghazal: Stuyvesant Cove Park*

Our cove, host to creatures feathered and furred, on a sliver
of shore, is south of East Twenty-third at the river.

The cove was there before there was a village green,
before tenements, before developers stirred, at the river.

Then known for boat building, meat packing,
      and gas houses,
now, secrets safe, artifacts rest interred at the river.

---

*The *ghazal* (pronounced ghuzzle) is a Persian poetic form made up of
couplets with a strict rhyme scheme and other requirements I have tried to
satisfy here.

In the seventies, cynics scoffed at the Park Proposal:
A park—in that space—how absurd. At the river

in the eighties, on tumbledown piers, we sunbathed.
Now burnt-out sticks show what occurred at the river.

It was carved from a wasteland, fought for by New Yorkers.
Even worms turning soil know a park's much preferred
        at the river.

Nostrils flaring, joggers, bikers, roller-bladers sniff salt and
offer thanks that the people's will was heard for the river.

In Chrysler spear, UN chunk, and (now our tallest)
        Empire State,
princes in their palaces are inferred at the river.

In panoramic stretches from here to Greenpoint, Brooklyn,
tugboats push barges (hope the pilot hasn't erred)
        at the river.

Round the bend, at Williamsburg, Manhattan, and
        Brooklyn bridges,
fishers' mem'ries of past catches are stirred at the river.

Shaded by native trees and shrubs, happy in
        plaid trousers,
good place to reminisce, folks concur at the river.

Up from the mayhem of FDR Drive, wings flapping,
black-backed gulls and geese to new heights are spurred
        at the river.

In rush-hour churning from ferries that fly to Wall Street,
lady crabs and clams are disturbed at the river.

On the shore, frilling with white, the slate-gray tidal waters,
sweet riffs purl the strand for man and bird at the river.

Listen as small waves, all aquiver, lap the tiny beach.
Bufflehead ducks dive, cormorants demur at the river.

Peg sees green treetops from her fourteenth-floor window
that Garland the Joy this park has conferred on our river.

CONTRIBUTING POETS

Rose Bernal has been writing poetry intermittently since the age of thirteen. She spent her working life as a full-time indexer in a publishing house but, since her retirement, has devoted herself to her main love: poetry. She spent two weeks at the Yeats International School in Ireland and has read in open sessions at various poetry venues around the city.

Esse Chasnoff has been writing since she was a little girl. She writes in her journal everyday, which is a source of new poems for her. She has attended New School writing courses and been a member of the Stuyvesant Cove poet's group since its inception.

Esther B. Cohen is a lifelong resident of New York City with her husband Morty, her children Nina and Paul, and grand-children Collin and Paul. She has been active in the arts community as artist, potter, and poet for over fifty years. The muse for her poem "Botticelli" is her beloved parrot.

Marilyn Driscoll is a native New Yorker and has been a Peter Cooper Village resident since 1975. After retiring from Ernst & Young, where she worked in personnel communications, Marilyn has directed her interests to devotional writing and poetry. In July 2006, Paulist Press will publish her book, *Devotions for Caregivers.*

Mary Fordham is a former children's wear designer, a lifelong learner, a periodic artist, a frequent environmentalist, an involved grandmother, a seasonal gardener, a yearly traveler, an aspiring goddess, a student of compassion, and an occasional poet.

Joy Garland is an environmental activist, a former science teacher, and the Executive Director of the Stuyvesant Cove Park Association. She was inspired by the Cove poets to try expressing her thoughts in poetry and to join their ranks. Joy, a native New Yorker, is the mother of Peter and Susan, the grandmother of Jarod and Heather, and the wife of Richard Garland.

Lynn Green has—as newspaper reporter, longtime business writer, creator and producer of screenplays, and poet—enjoyed a highly diverse career path. Her current projects include a feature-length film and a volume of poetry, which will be published in 2006.

Barbara Gurman had an active life in the business world. After her diagnosis of multiple sclerosis at the age of thirty-three, she counseled M.S. groups and ran spiritual and meditation groups. A divorce helped her "concentrate on being more of me," and poetry "always lifted her spirits to feel lighter and brighter."

Phoebe Hoss is by profession an editor of scholarly books. She has written poetry on and off all her life, particularly since her retirement in 1992. She has attended several poetry workshops at the New School and had several poems published. She has lived in New York City all her adult life, half of it in Stuyvesant Town.

Anne Lazarus is a retired teacher and an avid birder who is active in the Linnaean Society, a birding group. She writes occasionally for the Stuyvesant Cove Park Association newsletter, *The Cove*, and leads bird walks in the park.

Pamela Machado attended a progressive school in her early teens where she acted, wrote, and drew. In 1994, her husband died, and three years later, in connection with her volunteer job of reading to the blind and visually impaired at the Lighthouse, she joined a workshop in writing poetry. That set her on the path to writing poetry, as she has been doing ever since. She has also taken classes at the New School, and her poetry has appeared with that of other poets on three CDs.

David Mayer is a writer and artist, the author of a shot-by-shot analysis of Sergei Eisenstein's *Potemkin*, and a founder, with friends, of the Cinema Guild at the 92nd Street Y during the 1930s. He has worked in various media, including photography, pastels, clay, found objects, and poetry. Born in 1912, he is currently writing his memoirs of WWII.

Eve Nethercott. Light verse interested her first in the fifties, inspired by Richard Armour, Phyllis McGinley, and Ogden Nash. Her first love was serious poetry, but she found "lite verse" easier to write. However, in addition to her career as a graphic artist, her main creative endeavors were centered in watercolor painting and calligraphy, She studied art at Pratt Institute and the Art Students League, where she is a life member.

Stan Raffes is a retired social worker. He has been active in the New School writing program since his retirement, as well as in the poetry program at the Jefferson Market Library. Stan has had readings at both that library and the Fifth Avenue Presbyterian Church.

Dorothea Scher was born in Vienna in 1933 and arrived in the United States in 1939. She was always interested in writing, but turned to poetry in the late 1990s. In November 2005, she was asked to read at the Cornelia Street Cafe in Greenwich Village.

Judy Schermer has worked in the Arts for fifteen years, twelve at Lincoln Center. When she is captivated by a thought or event, she races to put it into poetry before it escapes, and when it reaches the written page, she learns what is lurking inside. She joined the United Nations where she was moved to photograph its multicultural reality. The work turned into the exhibition *"Exploring Diversity in Everyday Life"* put on view in the Secretariat to an audience of appreciative viewers.

Betsy Shepardson has developed her poetry through equine-facilitated therapy: the sensitivity of horses has tapped inner analysis and expression. She is a working writer and artist who is completing a Masters project in library and information science. She has previously written about the North American Indians in her poetry.

Alison Carb Sussman is a graduate of Sarah Lawrence College and New York University. She has written for the *The New York Times Book Review* and *Publishers Weekly*. Her poems have appeared in *The Anthology of Magazine Verse & Yearbook of American Poetry, California Quarterly, Clara Venus, fulva flava, Slipstream,* and other publications. She won two Amelia Awards for her poetry.

Peggy Unsworth was born in London but is now a naturalized American citizen. From 1970 to 1996, she taught a variety of grades and subjects at the United Nations International School. In retirement, she was active for several years in peer learning and teaching at the Institute of Retired Professionals at the New School in New York and at the Senior Academy of the University of South Florida.